Lerner SPORTS

SPORTS
ALL-STARS

ALEX MORGAN

Anthony K. Hewson

Lerner Publications ◆ Minneapolis

Lerner Publications Company
A division of Lerner Publishing Group, Inc.
241 First Avenue North
Minneapolis, MN 55401 USA

For reading levels and more information, look up this title at www.lernerbooks.com.

Main body text set in Albany Std.
Typeface provided by Agfa.

Library of Congress Cataloging-in-Publication Data
Names: Hewson, Anthony K., author.
Title: Alex Morgan / by Anthony K. Hewson.
Description: Minneapolis : Lerner Publications, [2020] | Series: Sports all-stars | Audience: Ages 7–11. | Audience: Grades K–3. | Includes bibliographical references and index.
Identifiers: LCCN 2018057300 (print) | LCCN 2019004521 (ebook) | ISBN 9781541556218 (eb pdf) | ISBN 9781541556119 (lb : alk. paper) | ISBN 9781541574465 (pb : alk. paper)
Subjects: LCSH: Morgan, Alex (Alexandra Patricia), 1989- —Juvenile literature. | Women soccer players—United States—Biography—Juvenile literature.
Classification: LCC GV942.7.M673 (ebook) | LCC GV942.7.M673 H48 2020 (print) | DDC 796.334092 [B] —dc23

LC record available at https://lccn.loc.gov/2018057300

Manufactured in the United States of America
1-CG-7/15/19

CONTENTS

The Gold Medal 4

Facts-at-a-Glance. 5

An Elite Athlete 8

Staying Fit 12

A Famous Face 16

Life at the Top 22

All-Star Stats 28

Source Notes 29

Glossary 30

Further Information 31

Index 32

GOLD MEDAL

Alex Morgan (middle) fights Canada for control of the ball in the 2012 Olympics.

The US Women's National Soccer Team was 4–0 heading into the semifinal against Canada during the 2012 Olympic Games. Just one more win and the Americans would play for the gold medal. It was a high-scoring game.

- **Date of Birth:** July 2, 1989

- **Position:** forward

- **League:** National Women's Soccer League (NWSL)

- **Professional Highlights:** won an Olympic gold medal in 2012; won the World Cup title in 2015 with the US Women's National Team; scored her 90th professional career goal in 2018

- **Personal Highlights:** wrote a series of children's books about soccer; got married in 2014; starred in a movie in 2018

Whenever Canada took the lead, the US team answered with a goal of its own. After 90 minutes, the game was tied 3–3.

The game went into overtime. After 30 extra minutes, neither team had scored. The **referee** added on three minutes at the end of the match. Time was running out. It was in the 123rd and final minute when Alex Morgan worked her magic.

Morgan was waiting near the goal. Her teammate Heather O'Reilly chased down the ball. Just before the ball went out of bounds, O'Reilly caught up and kicked it toward the goal. Canada defenders surrounded Morgan. But she rose above them, meeting the ball with her head and shooting it at the goal.

Morgan didn't even watch the ball go in the net. She just heard the roar of the

Morgan dribbles the ball down the field.

Morgan's header flies into the goal, winning the game for the United States.

crowd and knew she had done it. No US player had ever scored that late in a match.

A few seconds later, the final whistle blew. "I cried on the field—who does that?" Morgan said. "But it felt good. . . . We were going to the finals." Three days later, the United States won the gold medal.

Morgan scored 28 goals and had 21 **assists** that season. Only two other American women had scored more goals in one year. Morgan was named US Soccer Player of the Year and took third place for World Player of the Year. Those awards, along with her starring performance at the Olympics, showed how far Morgan had come. It showed that her years of practice and hard work were worth it.

AN ELITE ATHLETE

Alex has loved soccer since she was young.

Alex Morgan loved sports growing up. She played almost every sport she could. It was not unusual for her parents to take her from softball practice to soccer practice and then to a basketball game all in one day. But soccer became Alex's favorite because she loved to run.

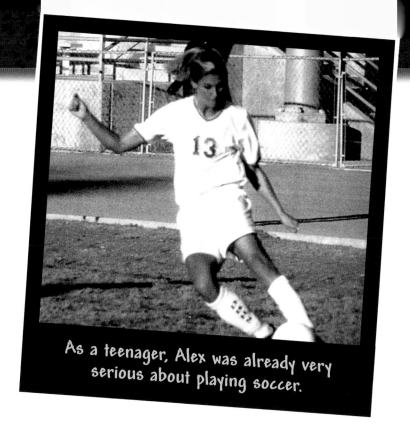

As a teenager, Alex was already very serious about playing soccer.

As a kid, Alex's soccer **idol** was Kristine Lilly. Lilly played in more international matches than anyone else in soccer history. Alex later wore Lilly's uniform number, 13.

Alex received her first US National Team experience in high school. At age 17, she began training with the national under-20 team. But her big moment was cut short when she tore the **anterior cruciate ligament (ACL)** in her right knee during practice. The injury forced her to miss a year of soccer, including most of her senior high school season.

Alex was a great student and athlete in college. She graduated from the University of California in three and a half years. She majored in political economy in industrialized societies.

When she recovered, Alex went on to play soccer at the University of California. She scored the most goals of any Golden Bears player in each of her four years on the team. During her senior year, she also helped the US National Team qualify for the Women's World Cup.

Alex made her Senior National Team **debut** on March 31, 2010. She played in eight matches for the National Team that year as a **substitute**. Alex made a big difference.

Alex celebrates a goal in a 2010 game against the Washington State Cougars.

She scored her first goal in a match against China on October 2. Then on November 20, she scored the game-winning goal against Italy in a match with a World Cup spot on the line.

Alex played a big role at the 2011 World Cup.

Alex takes a shot for the Portland Thorns during a 2014 game against the Washington Spirit.

She came off the bench in five of six matches. She scored two goals, and the US made it to the final. But that was just the start of what was to come.

Alex's performance at the 2012 Olympics made her an international star. She started playing in the National Women's Soccer League (NWSL) in 2013. After three seasons with the Portland Thorns, she was traded to the Orlando Pride in 2016. Morgan continued scoring goals, both for the Pride and the US National Team.

Morgan runs a lot to stay in shape.

Morgan plays forward. This means she has to be ready to run at all times. To keep her legs strong, Morgan does exercises that have her stop and start quickly.

Morgan does many different exercises to strengthen her body.

Running is a big part of Morgan's training. But she doesn't just run long distances. She changes the speed of her runs too. In one **routine**, she runs hard for two minutes and then jogs for one minute. She repeats this six times or more. Then she runs a mile and compares it to the amount of time it normally takes her to run a mile.

"The goal is to minimize the difference in times so I can be less **fatigued** in the 80th minute of a game," Morgan says.

Morgan practices with a soccer ball.

Morgan trains with many different exercises. She goes to **spin classes** and does yoga. Yoga improves her flexibility.

Besides exercising to stay in shape, Morgan practices her soccer skills too. Sometimes she practices with her team, but other times she practices alone.

Morgan practices **dribbling** the ball through cones. She also shoots off a wall to practice rebounds. Even the best players like Morgan practice these moves.

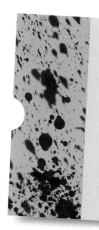

Soccer players are some of the fittest athletes in any sport. They can run as many as 10 miles in a single game.

Morgan strongly believes in drills. Practicing the same skills over and over makes it easier to use those skills during a game. Morgan is even featured in a smartphone app that has drills and instructional videos. The app helps young players practice by themselves.

Morgan also makes sure to eat healthfully. Banana pancakes are her favorite pregame food. She eats them about three hours before a game. This meal gives her energy. Nutrition is important in recovering from games too. Morgan eats food with protein 20 to 30 minutes after a game.

Morgan trains hard to stay fit for games.

Morgan poses on the red carpet at the ESPYs, an awards show from sports TV network ESPN.

Morgan's soccer fame has given her many opportunities off the field. She has appeared in magazines, television shows, video games, movies, and more. She has also **endorsed** many products from sporting goods to electronics.

UNICEF Kid Power gives kids points when they are active. The kids can then donate these points to help support local causes.

One of the ways Morgan uses her fame is to give back to the community. In 2016 Morgan teamed up with UNICEF, an organization that helps children around the world. Morgan joined the UNICEF Kid Power Team to help end global hunger.

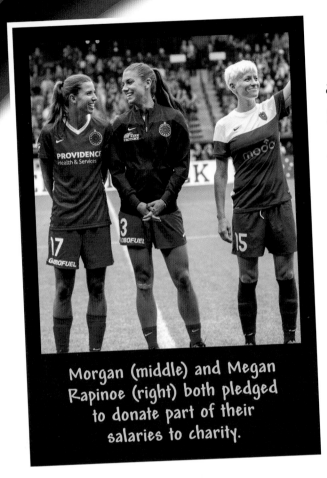

Morgan (middle) and Megan Rapinoe (right) both pledged to donate part of their salaries to charity.

In 2017 Morgan and US teammate Megan Rapinoe joined the Common Goal movement with other world soccer stars. Common Goal encourages players to donate part of their salaries to **charity**.

"As the global profile of women's [soccer] continues to grow, players like myself and Megan will have an increasing number of opportunities to use our status for good," Morgan said.

Morgan also tries to share her love of soccer with young people, especially young girls. In 2012 Morgan began writing a series of novels about the friendship of four girls and their shared love of soccer. The series is called The Kicks. Four books were planned. By 2018 she had written nine.

Morgan reached a new level of fame in 2015. She and the US National Team won the World Cup for the first time since 1999. The team was honored with a **ticker-tape** parade in New York City. They even got to meet President Barack Obama at the White House.

Morgan was a presenter at the 2015 ESPY Awards, where she and her US teammates won the award for Best Team.

Morgan held a book signing in New Jersey in 2013.

Morgan and her husband pose for a picture at the 2018 ESPYs.

That same year, Morgan was one of three women featured on the cover of the *FIFA 16* video game. It was the first time that women were featured on the cover of a *FIFA* video game. It was also the first edition of the game to feature women's teams, including the US National Team.

Morgan met her husband, pro soccer player Servando Carrasco, in college. They got married in 2014. Morgan's 2016 move to the Orlando Pride allowed her to stay close to her husband, who also played in Orlando. In 2018 he joined a different Major League Soccer team.

Off the field, Morgan likes to relax by watching TV or listening to music. Her favorite singers are Taylor Swift and Beyoncé.

Morgan (right) poses with costar Siena Agudong at the premiere of Alex & Me.

For her acting debut, Morgan had an easy role. It was herself. Morgan co-starred in the 2018 film *Alex & Me*. In the movie, Morgan plays a version of herself who comes to life from a poster in a fan's bedroom. Morgan said acting felt very different from playing soccer, but she enjoyed it.

Morgan (right) celebrates her 2012 Olympic gold medal with her team.

Morgan signs autographs for fans in 2012.

The world learned Morgan's name in 2011.

People soon knew she would be a star. In 2012 Morgan scored 28 goals, the greatest of her career.

Morgan also starred with her club team, the Seattle Sounders Women, in 2012. With Morgan, the Sounders had four times as many fans at their games than the next highest team. Morgan was only able to play in three matches with the Sounders because she was playing in the Olympics. But during those three matches she scored twice and had two assists.

The first NWSL team that Morgan played for was the Portland Thorns.

When the NWSL debuted in 2013, Morgan signed with the Portland Thorns. She scored in her first home game in front of a huge crowd of more than 16,000 fans.

"Seeing a full stadium out there today, standing on their feet the entire game, it gave me chills," Morgan said.

But a packed house in Portland was nothing compared to winning the World Cup in 2015. Morgan had struggled with injuries in 2014 and early 2015. She was working her way back when the World Cup games started. She scored just one goal. But she helped the United States win the World Cup.

Morgan took on a new challenge in 2017. During the off-season, she played with Lyon of France.

Morgan gets emotional as she celebrates winning the 2015 World Cup.

Morgan started playing for a French team in 2017.

Competing against the best teams in Europe, Lyon made it all the way to the Champions League final. Lyon won the championship, but Morgan was injured and had to miss most of the match.

Morgan scored the 90th goal of her professional career in the 2018 Tournament of Nations final, which the United States won. During her career, Morgan has helped the US Women's National Team win the two most important titles in soccer—Olympic gold and the World Cup.

Morgan is expected to have a long career ahead of her. She'll likely continue to be a leader on the US National Team. She hopes to lead the next generation of US stars to more worldwide glory.

Morgan kicks the ball while playing with the US National Team in a game against Canada.

All-Star Stats

Alex Morgan has scored a lot of goals in a pretty short time. Through 2018, here is where she ranked among the all-time leading goal scorers in US women's soccer:

Top Scorers in US Women's Soccer

1. Abby Wambach: 184
2. Mia Hamm: 158
3. Kristine Lilly: 130
4. Michelle Akers: 105
5. Carli Lloyd: 105
6. Tiffeny Milbrett: 100
7. Alex Morgan: 97
8. Cindy Parlow: 75

Source Notes

7. Alex Morgan, "Alex Morgan Recalls Thrilling 2012 Olympic Game Winner in New Book," *Sporting News*, June 4, 2015, http://www.sportingnews.com/us/soccer/news/alex-morgan-2012-olympics-canada-game-winning-goal-2015-womens-world-cup-book-breakaway/1cvefrp3zoia8191h7fb9hshtz

13. Lyndsay Green, "Steal Soccer Star Alex Morgan's World Cup Workout Regimen and Fitness Tips," *Teen Vogue*, April 28, 2015, https://www.teenvogue.com/story/soccer-pro-alex-morgan-world-cup-workout

18. Associated Press, "American Stars Morgan, Rapinoe Donating Salaries to Charity," *USA Today*, September 14, 2017, https://www.usatoday.com/story/sports/soccer/2017/09/14/american-stars-morgan-rapinoe-donating-salaries-to-charity/105594738

25. JonannaW, "Portland Thorns FC Match Recap: Reign Down, Roses Up," *Stumptown Footy*, April 22, 2013, https://www.stumptownfooty.com/2013/4/22/4254050/portland-thorns-fc-match-recap-reign-down-roses-up

Glossary

anterior cruciate ligament (ACL): a part of the knee that is commonly torn in sports injuries

assists: passes or rebounds from a teammate that lead directly to a goal

charity: an organization that helps other people or raises money for a good cause

debut: a first public appearance or performance

dribbling: moving the soccer ball up the field using one's feet

endorsed: supported or approved of someone or something, often while getting paid to do so

fatigued: feeling very tired

idol: someone who people admire

referee: someone who makes sure players follow the rules during a sports game

routine: a regular set of actions or way of doing things

spin classes: group exercise classes in which people pedal stationary bikes

substitute: a soccer player who sits on the bench until being called to replace a player on the field

ticker–tape: pieces of paper released into the air to celebrate

Further Information

Alex Morgan Official Website
http://alexmorgansoccer.com

Alex Morgan Orlando Pride Bio
https://www.orlandocitysc.com/players/53/alex-morgan

Alex Morgan US Soccer Bio
https://www.ussoccer.com/players/m/alex-morgan#tab-1

Fishman, Jon M. *Alex Morgan*. Minneapolis: Lerner
    Publications, 2016.

Jökulsson, Illugi. *Alex Morgan*. New York:
    Abbeville Kids, 2015.

Terp, Gail. *Alex Morgan*. Mankato, MN:
    Black Rabbit Books, 2017.

Index

acting, 21

Carrasco, Servando, 20

charity, 18

exercise, 12–14

FIFA 16, 20

food, 15

injuries, 9, 25–26

Olympic Games, 4–7, 11, 23, 27

Orlando Pride, 11, 20

Portland Thorns, 11, 25

Seattle Sounders Women, 23

University of California, 10

US Women's National Team, 4, 5, 6–7, 9–11, 19–20, 26–27

World Cup, 5, 10–11, 19, 25, 27

Photo Acknowledgments

The images in this book are used with the permission of: © Jamie McDonald/ FIFA/Getty Images, pp. 4–5, 7; © Stanley Chou/Getty Images Sport/Getty Images, p. 6; © Seth Poppel/Yearbook Library, pp. 8, 9; © Collegiate Images/ Getty Images, p. 10; © Tony Quinn/Icon SMI/Corbis/Icon Sportswire/Getty Images, p. 11; © David Madison/Getty Images Sport/Getty Images, pp. 12, 14; © Ronald Martinez/Getty Images Sport/Getty Images, p. 13; © Matthew Visinsky/Icon Sportswire/Getty Images, p. 15; © Jon Kopaloff/FilmMagic/Getty Images, p. 16; © Stephen Lovekin/UNICEF/Getty Images Entertainment/Getty Images, p. 17; © Diego Diaz/Icon Sportswire/Corbis/Getty Images, p. 18; © Dave Kotinsky/Getty Images Entertainment/Getty Images, 19; © Alberto E. Rodriguez/Getty Images Entertainment/Getty Images, p. 20; © Paul Archuleta/Getty Images Entertainment/ Getty Images, p. 21; © Michael Regan/Getty Images Sport/Getty Images, p. 22; © Leon Halip/Getty Images Sport/Getty Images, p. 23; © Brett Carlsen/Getty Images Sport/Getty Images, p. 24; © Kevin C. Cox/Getty Images Sport/Getty Images, p. 25; © Christopher Lee/Getty Images Sport/Getty Images, p. 26; © Lachlan Cunningham/ Getty Images Sport/Getty Images, p. 27.

Front Cover: © Ezra Shaw/Getty Images Sport/Getty Images.